Out and About Activity Book

Ghosts

By
Gillian Osband
Illustrations by
David Simonds

Contents

KINGFISHER BOOKS

Creaks and Groans

If you see a strange shape or hear odd noises in the night it could be something quite ordinary, or it could be . . . a ghost! Britain has more ghosts per square kilometre than any other country, so keep a look out.

Ghosts come in many forms – people, animals or objects. Some appear regularly, some just once. Some seek revenge or warn of danger, while others just relive happy times from their lives. Old houses or historical places are often linked with ghosts. Here are some you can visit.

Felbrigg Hall

Felbrigg Hall, near Cromer in Norfolk is haunted by one of the Windham family, who once owned it. According to members of the Ketton family, who took over the house, the ghostly figure regularly visited the library there. The Kettons never disturbed him though – they hoped to haunt the house one day too.

Lacock Abbey

One night in 1250 the Abbess of Lacock Abbey, near Chippenham in Wiltshire was startled to see a vision of her son William in her room. Her friends dismissed the vision as a dream – her son was fighting a Crusade in the distant Holy Land. Six months later the Abbess received news that her son had died in battle on the very day he had appeared to her.

A Dizzy Ghost

Queen Victoria's favourite Prime Minister, Benjamin Disraeli, lived for over 40 years at Hughenden Manor, near High Wycombe in Buckinghamshire. Since he died, in 1881, Disraeli's ghost has roamed the house and has been seen going down the cellar steps – perhaps to check up on the spirits!

Claydon House

Sir Edmund Verney, King Charles I's standard bearer was captured by Cromwell's men during the Civil War. He refused to surrender the standard so the Roundhead soldiers cut his hand off and killed him. Later, the King won back his standard, still grasped in Sir Edmund's severed hand. The hand was sent back to Sir Edmund's home – Claydon House in Buckinghamshire, but his body was never found. Sir Edmund's ghost has often been seen searching the house for his hand.

Ghosties, Ghosties Everywhere!

Some houses are haunted by one ghost, some by two, but Borley Rectory in Essex was a record-breaker! It was haunted by its builder – Reverend Henry Bull, a nun, a phantom coach, ringing bells, flying objects and ghostly graffiti.

The Rectory burnt to the ground in 1939 and a woman's bones were found in the ruins – perhaps they had once belonged to the ghostly nun.

How to Haunt Your Own House

To create the right atmosphere you need some spooky sound-effects. If you have a tape recorder you can record them – then play them back to give your friends a surprise.

Phantom Hooves

Use two empty yoghurt pots, one in each hand. Tap one then the other on a table to make a hollow clopping sound.

Terrifying Thunder

Hold a large sheet of stiff card by the edges and shake it back and forth so the middle wobbles, making thunder sounds.

A Phantom Army

Take a tin with a lid, and lots of stones. Put the stones in the tin, put the lid on and shake it. It sounds like a marching army.

3

Ghostly Kings

The ghosts of people who died horribly are often troublesome. Perhaps they are seeking revenge, or are just too troubled to rest peacefully. There are plenty of royal ghosts around and, sadly, many were victims of murder and treason. No wonder they are so restless!

A Gruesome End

Edward II died a very gruesome death at Berkeley Castle, Gloucester, in 1358. He was held prisoner there after being deposed from the throne, but his enemies wanted him out of the way. His gaolers tortured him to death but left no tell-tale marks on his body – it was impossible to tell how he died. On the anniversary of his death, his ghostly screams still ring through the castle.

Royal Protection

Henry VI was slaughtered in 1471 in the Tower of London during the Wars of the Roses, between the House of York and the House of Lancaster – to which Henry belonged.

Henry was kind and gentle, and his ghost still appears at Muncaster Castle in Cumberland where the Pennington family once gave him refuge. Descendants of the family believe the ghost still protects them.

Kings of the Castle

Of the 25 ghosts at Windsor Castle, Berkshire, three are kings. Henry VIII wanders around at night and disappears into a wall. Charles I, who was beheaded in 1649, often stands by the table in the library. But his ghost still has its head! George III used to wander around in his dressing gown, asking 'What? What? What?'. His ghost still haunts the library, muttering.

WHOOO... OHHH!!! OOOHHH!! ...ARGGH!!!

Moans

A game for any number.

Clear a space. Choose a ghost hunter and blindfold him. The other players (ghosts) circle around the ghost hunter who tries to catch one of them. If one is caught it must wail while the ghost hunter tries to guess who it is. If he is right, they change places, if not, he lets that ghost go and tries again.

Mix and Match Ghosts and Monsters

Create your own gruesome ghosts and menacing monsters . . .

You need: A spiral-bound notebook, scissors, a ruler, a pencil, crayons or felt-tip pens, a vivid imagination and nerves of steel.

Divide the first page of your notebook into three equal parts by drawing two lines across the page, as shown in the picture. Repeat this on about the first eight pages, making sure that you draw the lines in the same place on each page.

Draw your first gruesome creature on the first page with its head (always assuming it has one!) on the top third of the page, its body in the middle and its legs at the bottom. Draw a different ghost or monster on each page and colour them in.

Cut carefully along the lines on each page, so you can turn each third on its own. Now, by flipping the parts of the pages backwards and forwards you can mix up the different heads, bodies and legs to make even more horrific monsters.

... and Queens

There are plenty of ghostly queens around too, including some of the wives of Henry VIII. Again, many queens died as a result of some treachery and their spirits may therefore have good reason to wander among the living.

Anne Boleyn

Henry VIII was responsible for creating a number of queenly ghosts. He had his second wife, Anne Boleyn, beheaded on May 19th, 1536. On the anniversary she appears at Blickling Hall in Norfolk where she spent happy childhood days.

But her ghostly appearance is anything but cheerful. She is seen riding in a coach pulled by a headless horse, driven by a headless coachman, with her own head resting in her lap! After her coach enters the drive that leads to the hall the apparition slowly disappears.

Isabella's Yells

The ruined Castle Rising near King's Lynn, Norfolk was once the home of Queen Isabella of France, wife to the unfortunate Edward II. It seems she was a rather moody, bad-tempered woman, and her ghost is no improvement – her wailing and screaming can still be heard at night in the ruins.

1000 Year Old Ghost

Boudicca was the queen of an ancient tribe called the Iceni in the part of Britain now known as Norfolk. She led her armies against the invading Romans, but poisoned herself when she suffered defeat in AD 61. At Cammeringham village, north of Lincoln, near the Roman road known as Watling Street, Boudicca is sometimes seen at daybreak. She races by in a chariot, pulled by two horses, with her hair and gown streaming behind her.

A Ghostly Head

Many of the royal ghosts seem to have lost their heads in some way. You can impress your friends by having your own royal, ghostly 'head'.

You will need: a balloon, old newspapers, wallpaper paste, paints, a gold or silver paper cake frill, bits of wool, a piece of string or elastic.

Mix up the paste according to the instructions on the packet, and add bits of torn-up newspaper to make papier mâché. Blow the balloon up to about the same size as your head, then cover half of it with a layer of papier mâché. Make mouth and eye holes and add the other features. For example, a matchbox half for the nose.

Leave the mask to dry then paint the face, stick on the wool hair and cut the cake frill in half and stick it on as a crown. Burst the balloon and you should be left with a spooky mask. You can wear it yourself with string or elastic to hold it in place, or just hang it up in a dark corner, or so that it peeps through a window.

Let the papier mâché dry and then paint

Cut a matchbox from corner to corner for a nose

Stick on wool for hair

A Wild Dash

Catherine Howard, the fifth of Henry VIII's unfortunate wives, makes regular appearances at Hampton Court, where she is just one of at least a dozen ghostly inhabitants. When she was arrested there in 1541, accused of being unfaithful to the king, she rushed through the palace to plead with him. He did not want to be disturbed so the guards dragged her away. Her wild dash and her anguished cries can still be heard.

A Grateful Ghost

Sawston Hall near Cambridge is haunted by the ghost of Mary Tudor, who stayed there in 1553. The Duke of Northumberland wanted to take her prisoner and place his daughter-in-law, Lady Jane Grey on the throne. But John Huddleston, the owner of the hall smuggled Mary to safety dressed as a milkmaid. The Duke's men set fire to the hall, but Mary had it rebuilt and her ghost is often seen there.

Cursed Castles

Many castles have deep, dark secrets. Many castles have ghosts – and sometimes more than one. Next time you visit a castle try and find out something about its history. Then close your eyes and listen. You may just be able to hear whispers from the past.

The Knights' Night

Midsummer's Eve, June 20th, is a magical time when faeries and spirits roam freely. At Cadbury Castle in Somerset, there are strange happenings every seven years on that night. A 'door' is said to open on a hill inside the castle and King Arthur and his men ride out to water their horses near the church at Sutton Morris. Excavations have revealed remains of an ancient gate at the very spot where the ghostly knights appear!

Pop-up Ghost Card

You need: 2 pieces of stiff white paper or thin card, a paper drinking straw, sticky tape, a pencil, felt-tip pens, scissors.

1. Take one piece of paper and fold it round to make a cone shape, leaving a small hole at the bottom to fit the straw through. Tape the paper securely so it keeps its shape.

2. Trim the top to make it even, as shown here. Then make the cone look like a castle. Cut battlement shapes at the top, draw little windows and a portcullis and colour it all in.

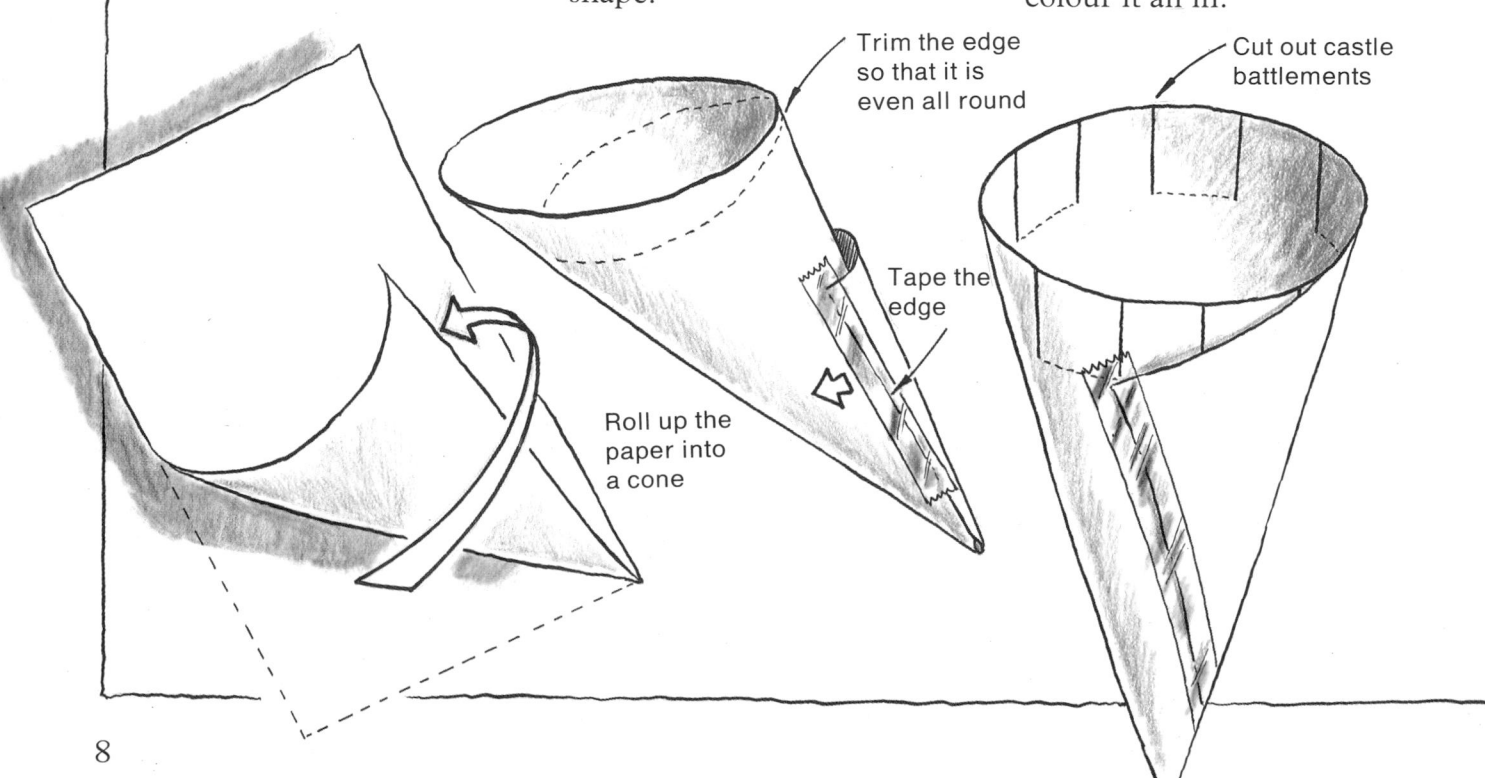

Roll up the paper into a cone

Trim the edge so that it is even all round

Tape the edge

Cut out castle battlements

Gloomy Glamis

The castle of Glamis, in Tayside is full of dark secrets, like the bloodstain which keeps reappearing on the spot where King Duncan was murdered by Macbeth in 1040.

One room has been sealed off for years. Some members of the Ogilvy clan once sought protection at Glamis from their enemies, the Lindseys, but the Earl of the time just locked them in the room and left them to starve. Their cries have often been heard since then.

It's Not Me!

HERE
LIES
ARTHUR
DARRELL
R.I.P.

The Puzzled Ghost

Scotney Castle, in Kent has two ghosts. The ghost of Arthur Darrell, owner of the castle in the 18th century, was seen at his own graveside muttering 'That is not me!' He was later proved right when his coffin was found to contain stones! The other ghost is of a customs officer killed by a smuggler and thrown into the castle moat. He rises from his watery grave, dripping mud, and hammers on the castle door.

3. On the second piece of paper draw a ghost shape, but make sure it is small enough to fit inside your castle. Colour it and cut it out. Tape the top part of the straw to the back of the ghost.

4. Fit the straw down through the hole in the bottom of the cone and pull it down so the ghost is hidden. When you push the straw up the ghost pops up to haunt your castle.

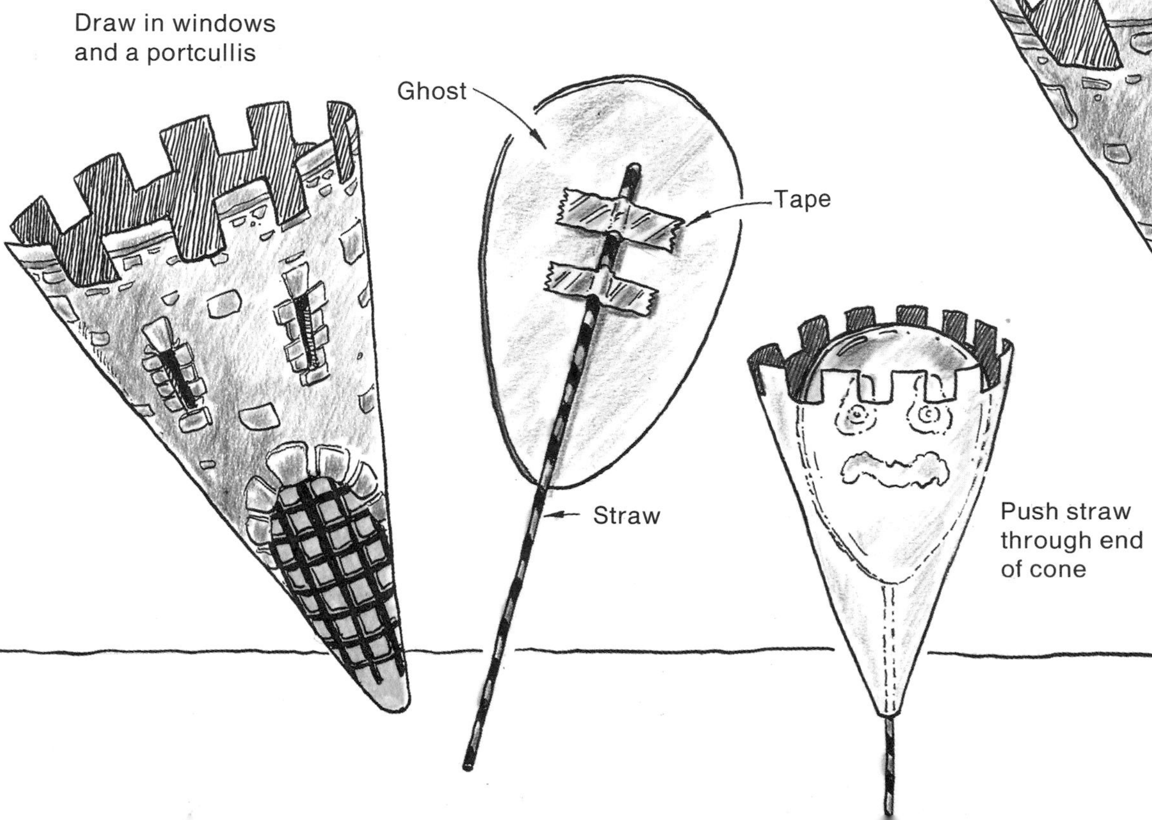

Draw in windows
and a portcullis

Ghost

Tape

Straw

Push straw
through end
of cone

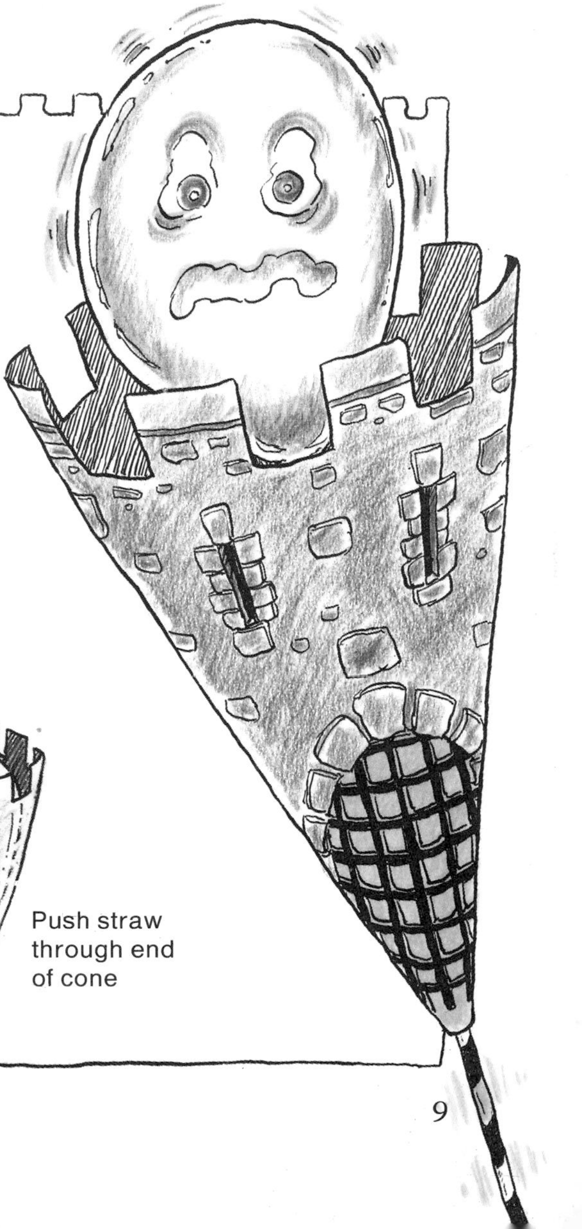

Chilling Children

Not all ghosts are adults. Plenty of kids have come back as ghosts to haunt the living. But being smaller doesn't make them any less scary.

In fact, if anything, they sometimes seem even more frightening than bigger spirits. Maybe these junior spooks will give you some extra ideas for haunting your own house!

A Horrible Hairy Hand

You need: an old rubber glove, dry sand, some thick black or brown wool, string, red ink, scissors, glue, old newspaper.

1. Spread newspaper over the floor or table.
2. Dip a piece of string about 15cm long in the red ink and leave it to dry.
3. Fill the glove with sand.
4. Tie the string around the wrist part of the glove to keep in the sand.
5. Glue bits of wool all over the glove to look like hair.
6. Once the glue has dried, you can leave your horrible hairy hand where someone will notice it. Arrange the ends of the string to look like trickles of blood. Yuk!

Repulsive Rhymes

Here is a fairly horrible rhyme.

A ghoul stood on the bridge
  one night,
Its lips were all a-quiver,
It gave a cough,
Its leg dropped off,
And floated down the river.

Can you invent a rhyme that is utterly disgusting? Have a competition with your friends, preferably after dark, with a full moon shining for ghostly inspiration.

The Little Princes

Edward and Richard were the sons of King Edward IV. After he died, Edward IV's brother, also called Richard, became the boys' guardian. When young Edward was about to be crowned, in 1483, the boys were taken to stay at the Tower of London.

Three assassins crept into their room and smothered them but to this day no-one knows who ordered their murder. The two young boys still haunt the Bloody Tower.

The Children of Bramber

Ruined Bramber Castle in West Sussex is haunted by a number of ghosts, but the saddest of all are the three children of the Norman lord, William de Breose.

King John suspected William was not loyal to him and took his children hostage in their own castle, where he starved them to death. The poor little ghosts are still to be seen there, some 800 years later, begging for food.

Spooky Scribbler

A poltergeist is a spirit that moves things around. How many words can you make by moving the letters of the word POLTERGEIST around? You don't have to use all the letters in each word, but you can only use each letter the same number of times it appears in the original word. Check your score on page 24.

Awful Animals

Animal ghosts are commoner than you might think. Although horrific horses (often headless) and daunting dogs (usually huge with strange glowing eyes) seem to be in the majority, there are other types. Even squirrels and hares may turn out to be more – or less – than they seem!

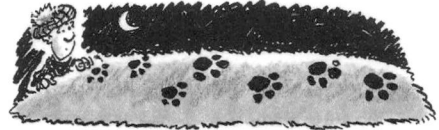

Demon Doggies

A huge phantom dog appears every year on January 4th on the road between Knockando and Milton of Auchriachan in the Scottish Highlands. It leaves tracks larger than a man's hand.

At Leeds Castle in Kent, a phantom black dog actually saved a life. A member of the family who once owned the castle was sitting in a bay window overhanging the moat, when she saw the black dog walk across the room and disappear. When the lady went to investigate, the bay where she had been sitting fell into the moat below!

Monkey Business

Athelhampton Hall, Dorset has been haunted by a most unusual animal since 1595! The Martyn family who lived there kept pet apes. One day the daughter, who had been jilted by her lover, ran off in tears through a secret passage leading from the library.

One of the pet apes followed her but she didn't notice, and when she closed the door it was shut in and starved to death. It haunts the passage to this day.

Furry Fiends

King John's Hunting Lodge in Axbridge, Somerset is famous for its phantom tabby cat which walks through closed doors. On one occasion the cat sat down, curled up and disappeared.

At Abbey House in Cambridge there have been sightings of a ghostly red squirrel which runs along a wall then vanishes, and of a mystery hare. The hare often appears when there is snow on the ground, but leaves no footprints. St Donat's Castle in South Wales has a more exotic spectral pet – a phantom panther!

Spooky Shadows

Scare your friends (and fiends) with beastly bats, horrifying hounds and screaming stallions. . .

You need: A lamp (a flexible desk lamp is best), a light coloured wall, your hands.

The best time to put on your show is . . . when it's dark. Shine the light on the wall – and off you go. Practise a bit beforehand, just to perfect your technique. The idea is to make shapes with your hands in front of the lamp so they cast shadows.

If you hold your hands close to the lamp and far from the wall, you end up with big shadows, but slightly out of focus. With your hands closer to the wall and further from the lamp, you get small, sharp shadows. Here are a few shapes to try.

Horrific Horses

A huge white, riderless stallion has been seen by many people at night on the roads around Charlbury in Oxfordshire. It terrifies drivers by leaping over hedges and charging across roads before disappearing.

The White Horse of Uffington in Berkshire can be seen by anyone. It is carved out of the turf on the hillside to show the chalk below. But once every one hundred years it is said to come to life and leave the hill, to be shod at Wayland's Smithy nearby. The last time this happened was about fifty years ago.

The Laidly Worm

Although the story of the Laidly Worm is not exactly a ghost story, it has many of the same ingredients – envy, magic, innocence, treachery, a horrifying apparition and the eventual victory of good over evil, helped along by love, bravery and trust. Altogether a good recipe for an adventure into the supernatural. It is set in the wilds of Northumberland, in Bamburgh Castle.

There was once a king who had a handsome son, Childe Wynd and a lovely daughter, Margaret. One day, his son went to seek his fortune and the king decided to travel south to go hunting.

The king had been lonely since the death of his wife, so when he met a beautiful lady on his travels he decided to marry her and take her home.

He did not realize that his new queen was a witch, who had made him fall in love with her by magic. He sent word of his marriage home.

Margaret was upset to hear she had a stepmother. When the new queen arrived she could not hide her feelings. The queen hated her at once.

14

The witch-queen decided she had to get Margaret out of the way. One night she stole down to the dungeons and cast a wicked spell. She turned Margaret into a horrible monster. The spell would only be broken if Childe Wynd, her brother, kissed the monster three times. Next morning, Margaret's maids came to wake her as usual.

To their horror they discovered a scaly, worm-like monster in her bed. They chased it from the castle to nearby Spindlestone Rock. Hunger drove the Laidly Worm to steal livestock. The local people were terrified and went to a warlock for advice.

He told them the worm was their own princess and that they should feed it the milk of seven cows each day. He also told them to find Childe Wynd at once. When Childe Wynd heard of the terrible monster he changed the rudder of his ship to one of rowan wood to protect him against the queen's magic and set sail for home. Soon dark clouds gathered and a terrible storm threatened Childe Wynd's ship nearly making it sink.

15

The queen knew Childe Wynd was drawing near and turned all her evil magic against him, but his piece of rowan protected him and he came ashore safely.

He wanted to kill the monster – he didn't believe it was Margaret. But it spoke to him, and when he saw a big tear roll down its face he knew the story was true.

He quickly gave it three kisses, as it asked. There was a terrible hiss and a roar and there before him stood Margaret once more. They were both overjoyed.

They made their way to the castle and found the witch-queen there all alone and in a furious temper. Childe Wynd touched her with the rowan and she turned into a toad.

If you ever visit Bamburgh Castle look out for the ugly little toad that still haunts the keep and dungeons to this day. I wonder if the wicked queen has learnt her lesson?

Maddening Monsters

There are many other monster tales from all over the world but one of the most famous is that of the Loch Ness Monster. There have been many sightings over the years and even one or two rather blurred photographs. But even with the most modern scientific equipment it has so far been impossible to prove (or disprove) that it exists. The loch, near Inverness in Scotland, is very deep and one theory is that prehistoric creatures left over from the distant past still live and breed there.

A Scary Bat

Although real bats are totally harmless you can exploit their undeserved bad reputation to give your friends a surprise.

You need: a sheet of thin card painted black on both sides, a pencil, scissors, old newspaper, and some black cotton.

Copy half the bat shape shown here onto a sheet of folded newspaper. Cut it out and open it up to give a whole bat shape. Draw round it onto the black card and cut the card carefully. Fold the card in half down the middle of the body then fold the wings back in a flight position.

If you make several bats you can hang them from the ceiling using the black cotton, or upside down by their feet.

Lost Lovers

Many love stories have had unhappy endings – so there are plenty of ghostly lovers wandering around seeking their lost partners, regretting their mistakes or cursing those who foiled their plans.

A Love Trap

In the 12th century, Ludlow Castle, Shropshire was thought to be unconquerable. Marion de la Bruere, who lived there, wanted to see her lover Arnold de Lys, but the castle was under siege. She lowered a rope for him to climb but got more than she bargained for. Arnold was one of the enemy, and brought 100 soldiers with him. When Marion realized this, she threw herself off the tower and her ghost has been seen falling from the window where she was betrayed.

The Ghostly Nun

In a street in Brighton you can see a bricked-up door that is no obstacle to a ghostly nun, who lived in the 12th century. She loved a soldier and they ran away together but were caught. The soldier was executed, and the nun was walled up and left to starve in a cell behind the old door. Sadly, her ability to walk through walls only developed after her death.

Supernatural Scramble

What has happened to these words? Perhaps a poltergeist has been messing around with them. Can you sort them all out? Answers on page 24.

HOGUL IRPSIT
NAPMOTH THOGS NEBEASH
PARIPOINTA STIGRETOPLE
REPSTEC
MEZOBI YOPOSK

A Watery Grave

In 1815, Britain was at war with France. A young Norfolk drummer boy, from Hickling Green, was in love with a girl from a nearby village. Her father outlawed their meeting as he did not want them to marry, but they used to meet in secret on a marshy islet called Swim Coots. As it was a cold winter, the drummer used to skate over the frozen water to meet his love, but by the middle of February a thaw had set in and the boy fell through the ice and drowned. On misty evenings in February, his drum roll can still be heard and he has sometimes been seen searching for his love across the marshes.

Creepy Castle Maze

To show you don't believe in ghosts, you have agreed to spend the night at CREEPY CASTLE – but when darkness falls you realize this was a terrible mistake!

Can you find the way out of the castle without being caught by one of its ghosts or ghouls?

Drops of Blood

One March night in 1566, David Rizzio, Mary Queen of Scots' Italian secretary, was murdered in Holyroodhouse Palace by a gang of Scottish nobles led by Mary's husband, Lord Darnley. Legend has it that drops of Rizzio's blood stained the floor of the Queen's apartment in the north-west tower of the palace, and however often these are rubbed away, they will reappear.

To make your own drops of blood, you need: red ink, blotting paper, newspaper, a paintbrush, scissors. Spread the newspaper out so as not to make a mess. Use the paintbrush to drip ink onto the blotting paper. Leave it to dry, cut the drops out and put them somewhere conspicuous.

Scary Skulls

Some skulls are scary – some are friendly. But how would you like to have a skull living in your house? The skulls in these stories often turned up at the most inconvenient moments and seemed to cause great panic among the living. I'm sure you can understand why.

The Calgarth Skulls

Wealthy Myles Phillipson owned most of the land around Lake Windermere in the Lake District during the 16th century. There was one small farm he didn't own and the owners – Kraster and Dorothy Cook – didn't want to sell. Phillipson falsely accused the Cooks of theft and as he was the magistrate, they didn't stand a chance.

The Cooks were sentenced to death but they laid a curse on the stolen land. Phillipson built his new home, Calgarth Hall on the Cooks' farm, but soon after, two skulls appeared on the bannisters at the top of the stairs.

No matter how often they were smashed or buried, they just kept reappearing. When Phillipson died the skulls laughed all night long. Once his family sold the hall the skulls finally left.

A Determined Skull

Burton Agnes Hall in Yorkshire is a beautiful Tudor mansion. Anne Griffiths, daughter of the man who built it, was attacked by robbers while out walking. On her death-bed she made her sisters promise to keep her skull in the house. But they were too upset to do as she asked. After the funeral appalling noises rang through the house. No-one knew why, so the sisters turned to the vicar.

He said they should keep their promise and when Anne's coffin was opened the head was already separate from the body and the hair and flesh had disappeared leaving a skull. This was taken back to the hall and the haunting stopped at once, but whenever people have tried to remove it the noises have started again.

Speggtacular Spooky Eggs

You need: an egg, a darning needle, a mixing bowl, used matches, thick black cotton, black and white poster paints, black paper, felt-tip pens.

First you need to blow the eggs to leave an empty shell. Do this by carefully piercing a hole in each end of the egg (not your fingers) with the needle. Try to make sure you pierce the yolk as you stick the needle in. Now hold the egg over a bowl put your mouth over the hole at the top and blow hard. This should force the contents of the shell out into the bowl underneath.

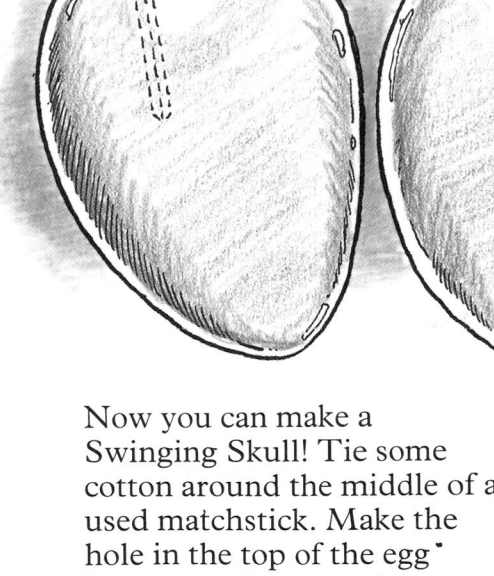

Now you can make a Swinging Skull! Tie some cotton around the middle of a used matchstick. Make the hole in the top of the egg large enough to put the match through. Jiggle the cotton so the match wedges across the inside of the egg and you can hang it up. Use the black and white paint to design a skull on your egg.

Or turn it into a Vile Vampire – paint the whole egg black and cut out bats' wings and feet from the black paper. Glue them on the shell and paint a scary vampire face. When the paint is dry you can hang the spooky egg up. It will look as if it is floating. Don't throw the inside of the egg away – make scrambled egg-toplasm!

Things That Go Bump

All sorts of things go bump in the night – so you can't just assume those strange noises are someone falling out of bed. Some ghosts never appear themselves, they just move things around or break things. This kind of ghost is known as a poltergeist. But there are also phantom objects (rather than people or animals) that make quite regular appearances. Which would you rather meet – a ghostly thing or a ghostly person?

A Fifty-year Wait

You will have to be patient to catch the next appearance of the schooner *Lady Luvibond* at Deal, Kent. It is seen once every 50 years and is next expected in 1998. It set sail from London in 1798 with the Captain's new wife on board. The first mate was in love with her and, in a fit of jealousy, deliberately wrecked the ship. Everyone on board was drowned. It seems that the phantom ship looks so real that in 1848, the Deal longshoremen set out to try and rescue the crew, but the ship simply disappeared.

Say it with Flowers

Near Widecombe-in-the-Moor, Devon is the grave of Mary Jay who hanged herself in a barn that once stood nearby. A man in a dark cloak has been sighted crouching at the head of her grave and fresh flowers have been known to appear there.

What a Performance!

The ghost of a woman who was hanged in Oxford in 1752 appeared at two places in Henley-on-Thames where a play about her was being produced. May Blandy's ghost switched lights on and broke mirrors in the town hall and the Kenton Theatre.

A Romantic Ghost

At Avebury Manor, Wiltshire, rose petals are regularly found strewn on the floor of one of the rooms, and locked doors and windows are mysteriously opened. A lady in white walks the grounds too, but no-one knows who she is.

Scented Spooks

At Cotehele, at Calstock in Cornwall, there have been many unexplained reports of a strong herbal fragrance that can suddenly be smelt and of the sound of ghostly music that comes from nowhere.

How Uplifting!

Sizergh Castle in Cumbria is haunted by a poltergeist that pulls up the floor boards in one of the rooms. Although they have been replaced several times the ghost keeps pulling them up.

A Phantom Bike

Cloud's Hill in Dorset was the home of Lawrence of Arabia. One night he had a fatal motorbike accident. Since then many people have heard the sound of a motorbike in the area.

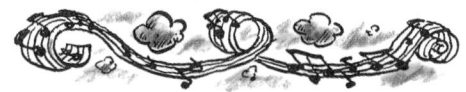

Ghostly Jokes

If you saw a werewolf, a vampire and a ghostly hound what would you do? *Pray you were at a fancy dress party.*

What is the best time to tell scary stories? *When the spirits move you.*

How do ghosts go through locked doors? *With a skeleton key.*

Did you hear about the stupid ghost? *It climbed over a wall.*

Why do vampires brush their teeth? *To prevent bat breath.*

What did the mother ghost say to the baby ghost? *Don't spook until you're spoken to.*

What did the little girl say to the ghost of Charles I? *You must be off your head.*

Ghost 1: I find haunting a real drag these days.
Ghost 2: Me too. I just don't seem to be able to put any life into it.

What is a ghost's most favourite food? *Spookghetti and ghoulash.*

Answers

Page 11: Spooky Scribbler
Check your score – how do you rate?
Below 30 – Cheat if necessary!
30 to 100 – Now you're getting somewhere. It's easy really.
100 to 200 – Impressive, You must be using hidden powers (or a dictionary).
200 to 300 – Terrifyingly brilliant.

Page 18: Supernatural Scramble
How many words did you unscramble?

Ghoul	Phantom
Spirit	Ghost
Poltergeist	Spectre
Apparition	Zombie
Spooky	Banshee

Kingfisher Books, Grisewood & Dempsey Ltd, Elsley House, 24–30 Great Titchfield Street, London W1P 7AD.

First published in 1989 by Kingfisher Books in association with The National Trust
10 9 8 7 6
Text Copyright © Gillian Osband 1989
Illustrations Copyright © David Simonds 1989

BRITISH LIBRARY CATALOGUING IN PUBLICATION DATA
Osband, Gillian
 Ghosts
 1. Great Britain. Ghosts
 I. Title II. Simonds, David
 III. Series
 133.1'0941
 ISBN 0 86272 421 X

Edited by Meg Sanders
Designed by Ben White
Cover design by David Jefferis
Phototypeset by Southern Positives and Negatives (SPAN), Lingfield, Surrey
Printed in Spain